CCDP Exam Prep - Designing Networks with Confidence

Table of Contents

Chapter 1: Introduction to CCDP Certification

Tutorial: Understanding CCDP Certification

Welcome to Chapter 1 of "Designing Networks with Confidence: A Comprehensive Guide to CCDP Exam Prep." In this chapter, we will introduce you to the Cisco Certified Design Professional (CCDP) certification and provide you with an overview of its benefits, prerequisites, and exam details.

What is CCDP Certification?

The CCDP certification is a professional-level certification offered by Cisco Systems that validates your knowledge and skills in designing advanced network infrastructures. It focuses on network design principles, methodologies, and best practices, preparing you to tackle complex design challenges and make informed decisions while designing enterprise-level networks.

Benefits of CCDP Certification:

Enhanced Career Opportunities: Obtaining CCDP certification opens up new career opportunities in network design and architecture. It demonstrates your expertise and proficiency in designing scalable, secure, and resilient network solutions.

Industry Recognition: CCDP certification is widely recognized and respected in the networking industry. It establishes you as a qualified professional with the ability to design complex network infrastructures.

Increased Professional Credibility: By earning CCDP certification, you gain credibility among colleagues, employers, and clients. It validates your skills and knowledge, enhancing your professional reputation.

Prerequisites for CCDP Certification:

To pursue CCDP certification, you need to meet the following prerequisites:

CCNA Routing and Switching or CCIE certification: You must have a valid CCNA Routing and Switching certification or any CCIE certification as a prerequisite.

CCDA Certification: Before attempting the CCDP exams, you need to earn the Cisco Certified Design Associate (CCDA) certification, which covers fundamental network design concepts.

CCDP Exam Details:

The CCDP certification consists of three exams:

300-320 ARCH: Designing Cisco Network Service Architectures

Duration: 75 minutes

Question Format: Multiple choice, drag and drop, simulations

Topics Covered: Designing advanced addressing and routing, network services, network security, and network management.

300-325 DEVDNLD: Designing Cisco Enterprise Networks

Duration: 90 minutes

Question Format: Multiple choice, drag and drop, simulations

Topics Covered: Designing advanced enterprise campus networks, enterprise edge, WAN, and security.

300-330 DENTAL: Designing Cisco Data Center Infrastructure

Duration: 90 minutes

Question Format: Multiple choice, drag and drop, simulations

Topics Covered: Designing data center infrastructure, data center storage networks, and data center virtualization.

Passing all three exams is required to achieve CCDP certification.

Conclusion:

In this tutorial, we introduced you to the CCDP certification and provided an overview of its benefits, prerequisites, and exam details. CCDP certification enhances your career opportunities, earns you industry recognition, and increases your professional credibility. Remember, acquiring a CCDA certification is a prerequisite, and you need to pass three exams to become a CCDP-certified professional.

In the upcoming chapters, we will delve into the world of network design principles, methodologies, and various design considerations. So, let's get started on your journey to becoming a proficient CCDP-certified professional!

Chapter 2: Design Principles and Methodologies

Tutorial: Understanding Network Design Principles

Welcome to Chapter 2 of "Designing Networks with Confidence: A Comprehensive Guide to CCDP Exam Prep." In this chapter, we will explore the fundamental network design principles and methodologies that are essential for creating effective and scalable network architectures.

Why are Design Principles Important?

Design principles provide a structured approach to network design, ensuring that networks are efficient, scalable, secure, and resilient. By adhering to design principles, you can create networks that meet business requirements, accommodate future growth, and deliver optimal performance.

Let's dive into some key network design principles:

Modularity:

Modularity involves breaking down a network into smaller, independent modules. This approach simplifies network management, enhances scalability, and allows for easier troubleshooting. Modularity enables you to add or remove network components without disrupting the entire network.

Hierarchy:

Hierarchy is the organization of network components in a layered structure. This approach promotes scalability and simplifies network design and management. A hierarchical design typically consists of core, distribution, and access layers, each with its own set of functions and responsibilities.

Resiliency:

Resiliency refers to the network's ability to recover quickly from failures and continue operating smoothly. Redundancy plays a crucial role in achieving resiliency. By implementing redundant components, such as backup links, power supplies, and devices, you can minimize network downtime and ensure high availability.

Scalability:

Scalability is the network's capability to accommodate growth and increased traffic demands. When designing a network, it's important to consider future expansion and the ability to handle additional users, devices, and applications. Scalable networks are flexible and can adapt to changing business requirements.

Security:

Network security is a critical aspect of any design. It involves implementing measures to protect the network from unauthorized access, data breaches, and other security threats. Consider incorporating technologies such as firewalls, intrusion detection systems (IDS), and secure remote access solutions into your design.

Network Design Methodologies:

Several methodologies can guide you through the network design process. Two widely used methodologies are:

Cisco Enterprise Architecture:

Cisco Enterprise Architecture is a comprehensive approach to network design that encompasses the entire enterprise network. It includes the Enterprise Campus, Enterprise Edge, Enterprise Data Center, and WAN modules. This methodology provides a structured framework for designing robust and scalable enterprise networks.

PPDIOO (Prepare, Plan, Design, Implement, Operate, Optimize):

PPDIOO is a lifecycle approach to network design that consists of six phases. Each phase involves specific activities and tasks, ensuring a systematic and well-structured design process. Following the PPDIOO methodology helps create networks that align with business requirements and are easier to manage and troubleshoot.

Conclusion:

In this tutorial, we explored the fundamental network design principles and methodologies that form the foundation of effective network architectures. Design principles such as modularity, hierarchy, resiliency, scalability, and security are crucial for creating networks that meet business needs and provide optimal performance. Additionally, methodologies like Cisco Enterprise Architecture and PPDIOO guide you through the network design process in a systematic manner.

In the next chapter, we will delve deeper into network design models and architectures, including campus networks, data centers, WANs, and remote connectivity. So, let's continue on our journey to mastering CCDP certification and becoming skilled network designers!

Chapter 3: Network Design Models and Architectures

Tutorial: Exploring Network Design Models and Architectures

Welcome to Chapter 3 of "Designing Networks with Confidence: A Comprehensive Guide to CCDP Exam Prep." In this chapter, we will delve into various network design models and architectures commonly used in enterprise environments. Understanding these models and architectures is crucial for designing robust and efficient networks.

Campus Network Design:

Campus networks form the foundation of an enterprise network, connecting end-user devices and providing access to network resources. When designing a campus network, consider the following factors:

Access Layer: This layer provides connectivity to end-user devices, such as computers, phones, and printers. Design considerations include access control, VLAN segmentation, and Power over Ethernet (PoE) for IP phones and wireless access points.

Distribution Layer: The distribution layer aggregates traffic from multiple access switches and provides routing, filtering, and policy enforcement. It ensures efficient communication within the campus network and connectivity to external networks.

Core Layer: The core layer provides high-speed switching and routing between distribution switches. It should be designed for high availability and low latency to ensure optimal performance.

Data Center Design:

Data centers house critical servers, storage systems, and networking equipment. When designing a data center network, focus on the following aspects:

Network Segmentation: Segment the network into different zones based on the sensitivity of data and security requirements. Use firewalls and access control mechanisms to control traffic flow between zones.

Storage Networks: Design and implement storage area networks (SANs) to facilitate efficient storage access and data replication. Technologies such as Fibre Channel and iSCSI are commonly used for storage networking.

Virtualization: Consider implementing virtualization technologies such as VMware or Hyper-V to consolidate servers and maximize resource utilization. Virtualized networks and software-defined data centers are becoming increasingly popular.

Wide Area Network (WAN) Design:

WANs connect geographically dispersed locations and provide connectivity to remote sites. Consider the following aspects when designing a WAN:

Connection Types: Evaluate different connection options, such as leased lines, MPLS (Multiprotocol Label Switching), Ethernet, and Internet VPNs. Each option has its own benefits and considerations.

Bandwidth and QoS: Determine the required bandwidth for each site and implement Quality of Service (QoS) mechanisms to prioritize critical traffic, ensuring optimal performance for applications such as VoIP or video conferencing.

Redundancy: Design redundant WAN links to provide high availability and fault tolerance. Technologies such as link aggregation, hot standby routers, and dynamic routing protocols can be utilized for redundancy.

Remote Connectivity and VPN Design:

Designing secure remote connectivity is essential for enabling remote access to the corporate network. Consider the following aspects:

Remote Access Technologies: Evaluate technologies such as VPNs (Virtual Private Networks), SSL (Secure Sockets Layer), IPsec (Internet Protocol Security), and remote desktop solutions. Choose the appropriate technology based on security requirements and user needs.

Authentication and Authorization: Implement strong authentication mechanisms, such as two-factor authentication, to ensure secure remote access. Use role-based access control (RBAC) to control user permissions.

Security Considerations: Design the remote connectivity solution with security in mind. Implement encryption, intrusion detection/prevention systems, and access control policies to protect against unauthorized access and data breaches.

Conclusion:

In this tutorial, we explored various network design models and architectures, including campus networks, data centers,

WANs, and remote connectivity. Understanding the design considerations and requirements for each architecture is crucial for creating robust, scalable, and secure networks. Consider factors such as access layer, distribution layer, core layer for campus networks; network segmentation, storage networks, and virtualization for data centers; connection types, bandwidth, and redundancy for WANs; and remote access technologies, authentication, and security for remote connectivity.

In the next chapter, we will focus on designing for high availability and fault tolerance. So, let's continue our journey to mastering CCDP certification and becoming skilled network designers!

Chapter 4: Designing for High Availability and Fault Tolerance

Tutorial: Creating Resilient Network Designs

Welcome to Chapter 4 of "Designing Networks with Confidence: A Comprehensive Guide to CCDP Exam Prep." In this chapter, we will explore the principles of designing for high availability and fault tolerance. Building resilient network designs ensures that your network can withstand failures and maintain uninterrupted operation. Let's dive in!

Redundancy and Device Failure:

Redundancy involves duplicating critical network components to eliminate single points of failure. When designing for high availability, consider the following:

Redundant Links: Implement multiple physical or logical links between devices to provide backup paths. Technologies such as EtherChannel or link aggregation can be used to bundle multiple links and increase available bandwidth.

Redundant Devices: Deploy redundant network devices, such as routers, switches, or firewalls, to ensure device-level fault tolerance. Use protocols like Hot Standby Router Protocol (HSRP) or Virtual Router Redundancy Protocol (VRRP) to create active/standby device pairs.

Power Redundancy: Consider providing redundant power supplies or backup power sources, such as uninterruptible power supplies (UPS), to prevent network outages due to power failures.

High Availability at the Network Layer:

To achieve high availability at the network layer, focus on the following design considerations:

Network Topology: Design a topology that enables redundant paths and eliminates single points of failure. For example, use a mesh or dual-homed design to ensure multiple paths between devices.

Routing Protocols: Implement dynamic routing protocols, such as Open Shortest Path First (OSPF) or Border Gateway Protocol (BGP), with proper tuning to enable fast convergence and optimal path selection.

Fast Convergence: Configure features like Bidirectional Forwarding Detection (BFD), Fast Link Pulses (FLP), or optimized timers to detect and recover from link or device failures quickly.

Load Balancing and Link Redundancy:

Load balancing distributes network traffic across multiple links, ensuring optimal utilization and preventing congestion. Consider the following techniques:

Equal-Cost Multipath (ECMP): Use routing protocols that support ECMP to distribute traffic across multiple paths with equal cost. This approach improves performance and provides redundancy.

Link Load Balancing: Implement technologies like link-state tracking or per-packet load balancing to evenly distribute traffic across available links.

Hot Standby Links: Configure hot standby links that remain idle until a primary link fails. This design ensures seamless failover and minimal disruption.

Fault Tolerance for Network Services:

Network services, such as DHCP, DNS, and NTP, play a crucial role in network operations. Ensure fault tolerance for these services by:

Redundant Servers: Deploy multiple servers for critical network services and implement mechanisms like load balancing or active/standby configurations.

Backup and Monitoring: Regularly back up service configurations and databases to ensure data integrity. Monitor service availability and performance to detect and resolve issues proactively.

Scalability: Design network service architectures that can accommodate future growth and increased demand. Consider factors like server capacity, network bandwidth, and fault tolerance mechanisms.

Conclusion:

In this tutorial, we explored the principles of designing for high availability and fault tolerance. By implementing redundancy, device failover, load balancing, and fault-tolerant network services, you can create resilient network designs that minimize downtime and ensure uninterrupted network operation. Consider redundant links and devices, power redundancy, and redundant service architectures. Also, focus on network layer high availability, fast convergence, load balancing techniques, and fault-tolerant network services.

In the next chapter, we will delve into advanced routing and switching design considerations. So, let's continue our journey to mastering CCDP certification and becoming skilled network designers!

Chapter 5: Advanced Routing and Switching Design

Tutorial: Designing Scalable and Secure Networks

Welcome to Chapter 5 of "Designing Networks with Confidence: A Comprehensive Guide to CCDP Exam Prep." In this chapter, we will explore advanced routing and switching design considerations. These concepts are essential for creating scalable, secure, and efficient network architectures. Let's get started!

Scalable Routing Architectures:

Scalable routing designs ensure that networks can handle increasing traffic demands and accommodate growth. Consider the following aspects:

Hierarchical Routing: Divide the network into routing domains using techniques like route summarization and Virtual Routing and Forwarding (VRF) instances. This approach reduces the size of routing tables and improves routing efficiency.

Route Redistribution: Implement proper route redistribution between routing protocols to enable seamless communication across different routing domains. Take care to prevent routing loops and ensure route stability.

Scalable Interior Gateway Protocols (IGPs): Utilize IGPs such as OSPF or Intermediate System to Intermediate System (IS-IS) for large-scale networks. These protocols offer features like area design, route summarization, and fast convergence.

Multicast and IPv6 Design:

Multicast and IPv6 are crucial components of modern network designs. Consider the following design considerations:

Multicast Design: Implement multicast routing protocols like Protocol Independent Multicast (PIM) to enable efficient delivery of multicast traffic. Design multicast distribution trees and use technologies like Multicast Source Discovery Protocol (MSDP) for inter-domain multicast communication.

IPv6 Integration: Design networks that support both IPv4 and IPv6 protocols. Consider aspects like dual-stack implementation, IPv6 addressing schemes, and IPv6 routing protocols such as OSPFv3 or Border Gateway Protocol (BGP) for IPv6.

Traffic Engineering and Quality of Service (QoS):

Designing networks that prioritize and manage traffic effectively is crucial for optimal performance. Consider the following aspects:

Traffic Engineering: Implement technologies like Traffic Engineering with Multiprotocol Label Switching (MPLS-TE) to optimize network resource utilization and provide efficient traffic flows across the network.

Quality of Service (QoS): Design QoS policies to prioritize critical applications and ensure appropriate bandwidth allocation. Utilize mechanisms like traffic classification, queuing, and traffic shaping to manage congestion and optimize performance.

Class of Service (CoS): Employ CoS mechanisms, such as Differentiated Services (DiffServ), to provide differentiated treatment for various types of traffic based on their importance or priority.

Layer 2 and Layer 3 Security Design:

Security is a critical aspect of network design. Consider the following design considerations for securing your network:

Access Control: Implement mechanisms like access control lists (ACLs), VLAN segmentation, and port security to control access and prevent unauthorized network access.

VLAN Design: Design VLANs that provide isolation and segmentation, enhancing security. Implement technologies like Private VLANs (PVLANs) to further restrict communication between devices.

Layer 3 Security: Utilize technologies like IPsec VPNs for secure communication across public networks. Implement security features like Control Plane Policing (CoPP) and routing protocol authentication to protect against attacks.

Conclusion:

In this tutorial, we explored advanced routing and switching design considerations, including scalable routing architectures, multicast and IPv6 design, traffic engineering, and Quality of Service (QoS). Additionally, we discussed layer 2 and layer 3 security design aspects to ensure network security. By implementing scalable routing, supporting multicast and IPv6, optimizing traffic management, and incorporating robust security measures, you can create networks that are efficient, secure, and capable of handling evolving business needs.

In the next chapter, we will dive into network services design, including DHCP, DNS, NTP, and network address translation (NAT). So, let's continue our journey to mastering CCDP certification and becoming skilled network designers!

Chapter 6: Network Services Design

Tutorial: Designing Reliable and Efficient Network Services

Welcome to Chapter 6 of "Designing Networks with Confidence: A Comprehensive Guide to CCDP Exam Prep." In this chapter, we will explore the design considerations for network services. Network services such as DHCP, DNS, NTP, and network address translation (NAT) are vital for efficient and reliable network operations. Let's dive into designing reliable and efficient network services!

DHCP (Dynamic Host Configuration Protocol) Design:

DHCP enables automatic IP address assignment and configuration for devices on a network. Consider the following design aspects:

DHCP Scopes: Design DHCP scopes based on network segments and requirements. Define IP address ranges, subnet masks, lease durations, and DHCP options.

Redundancy: Implement DHCP server redundancy using technologies such as DHCP failover or clustering to ensure uninterrupted IP address assignment.

IP Address Management (IPAM): Consider integrating IPAM solutions to centrally manage and track IP address assignments, monitor lease utilization, and streamline IP address management.

DNS (Domain Name System) Design:

DNS translates domain names into IP addresses, enabling users to access resources on the network. Consider the following design considerations:

DNS Hierarchy: Design a hierarchical DNS structure with primary and secondary DNS servers. Distribute DNS queries efficiently and ensure fault tolerance.

Caching: Utilize DNS caching to improve performance and reduce DNS query response times. Configure DNS servers to cache frequently accessed records.

DNS Security: Implement DNSSEC (DNS Security Extensions) to protect against DNS spoofing and ensure data integrity. Configure access control mechanisms to prevent unauthorized zone transfers.

NTP (Network Time Protocol) Design:

NTP synchronizes the time across devices on the network. Consider the following design aspects:

NTP Servers: Designate reliable NTP servers within the network or use public NTP servers. Ensure synchronization accuracy and reliability across the network.

Time Zones and Localization: Consider time zone requirements for geographically distributed networks. Configure NTP servers to support accurate time synchronization for different regions.

Authentication: Implement NTP authentication to ensure time accuracy and prevent unauthorized access or tampering.

Network Address Translation (NAT) Design:

NAT enables private IP addresses to be translated to public IP addresses, facilitating connectivity to the internet. Consider the following design considerations:

NAT Types: Choose the appropriate NAT type based on network requirements, such as static NAT, dynamic NAT, or port address translation (PAT).

Addressing Scheme: Design IP address allocation schemes for NAT, considering the number of required public IP addresses, address exhaustion concerns, and scalability.

NAT Logging and Monitoring: Implement NAT logging and monitoring mechanisms to track and analyze NAT translations, detect suspicious activities, and troubleshoot connectivity issues.

Network Management and Monitoring Design:

Efficient network management and monitoring are essential for maintaining network performance and detecting issues. Consider the following design considerations:

Network Management Protocols: Select appropriate protocols such as Simple Network Management Protocol (SNMP), NetFlow, or IPFIX to gather network performance and traffic data for monitoring and analysis.

Network Management Tools: Deploy network management tools that provide comprehensive monitoring, configuration management, and performance analysis capabilities.

Security and Access Control: Implement access control mechanisms for network management systems to ensure authorized access and prevent unauthorized configuration changes.

Conclusion:

In this tutorial, we explored the design considerations for network services, including DHCP, DNS, NTP, and NAT. By designing reliable and efficient network services, you ensure seamless IP address management, accurate name resolution, synchronized time, and connectivity to the internet. Consider DHCP scopes, DNS hierarchy, NTP server selection, NAT types, and network management and monitoring tools to optimize network services.

In the next chapter, we will focus on network integration and security, including integrating network components and implementing secure network designs. So, let's continue our journey to mastering CCDP certification and becoming skilled network designers!

Chapter 7: Network Integration and Security

Tutorial: Integrating Components and Implementing Secure Network Designs

Welcome to Chapter 7 of "Designing Networks with Confidence: A Comprehensive Guide to CCDP Exam Prep." In this chapter, we will delve into network integration and security considerations. Integrating network components effectively and implementing secure network designs are crucial for creating robust and protected network infrastructures. Let's explore the key concepts and design practices!

Integration of Network Components:

Integrating network components ensures seamless communication and optimal performance. Consider the following integration aspects:

Network Services Integration: Integrate network services such as DHCP, DNS, NTP, and authentication services like RADIUS or TACACS+ to provide centralized and efficient service delivery.

Application Integration: Ensure seamless integration of network-dependent applications by considering factors like network bandwidth, latency, and security requirements.

API Integration: Leverage Application Programming Interfaces (APIs) to integrate different network components, allowing for automation and orchestration of network processes.

Secure Network Design Best Practices:

Designing secure networks is essential to protect against unauthorized access, data breaches, and other security threats. Consider the following best practices:

Defense in Depth: Implement multiple layers of security, including perimeter security (firewalls, intrusion prevention systems), network segmentation, and host-level security measures (antivirus, host-based firewalls).

Secure Remote Access: Establish secure remote access mechanisms like VPNs with strong encryption, multifactor authentication, and access control mechanisms to protect against unauthorized access.

Network Segmentation: Divide the network into logical segments using VLANs, virtual routing and forwarding (VRF), or virtual private networks (VPNs) to isolate sensitive data and limit lateral movement of threats.

Identity and Access Management: Implement identity management solutions, role-based access control (RBAC), and strong authentication mechanisms to control user access and prevent unauthorized activity.

Network Access Control and Identity Management:

Network access control and identity management play a vital role in ensuring secure network operations. Consider the following design considerations:

Network Access Control (NAC): Implement NAC solutions to enforce security policies, validate the security posture of connecting devices, and provide granular access control based on device health and user credentials.

AAA Services: Configure Authentication, Authorization, and Accounting (AAA) services like RADIUS or TACACS+ to centralize user authentication and access control across the network.

Identity Services: Utilize identity services such as Active Directory or Lightweight Directory Access Protocol (LDAP) for centralized user management, authentication, and policy enforcement.

Network Segmentation and Isolation:

Segmenting and isolating the network enhances security and reduces the impact of security breaches. Consider the following design practices:

VLAN Segmentation: Design VLANs to separate traffic based on security requirements and functional needs, preventing unauthorized access to sensitive resources.

Virtual Routing and Forwarding (VRF): Implement VRF instances to create logical network segments with isolated routing tables, enhancing security and providing separation between different user groups or departments.

Guest Network Isolation: Design guest networks with restricted access and limited connectivity to ensure separation from the internal network, protecting internal resources from potential threats.

Conclusion:

In this tutorial, we explored network integration and security considerations. By effectively integrating network components, implementing secure network designs, and focusing on network access control and identity management, you can create robust and protected network infrastructures. Consider aspects such as network services integration, secure network design best practices, network access control, and network segmentation and isolation.

In the next chapter, we will discuss virtualization and cloud design, including virtualized network environments, cloud computing, and hybrid/multi-cloud network design considerations. So, let's continue our journey to mastering CCDP certification and becoming skilled network designers!

Chapter 8: Virtualization and Cloud Design

Tutorial: Designing Networks for Virtualized and Cloud Environments

Welcome to Chapter 8 of "Designing Networks with Confidence: A Comprehensive Guide to CCDP Exam Prep." In this chapter, we will explore the design considerations for virtualization and cloud environments. With the rise of virtualization and cloud computing, understanding how to design networks for these environments is crucial. Let's delve into the key concepts and design practices!

Virtualization Technologies and Concepts:

Virtualization enables the creation of virtual instances of servers, storage, and networking resources. Consider the following concepts and technologies:

Server Virtualization: Implement technologies such as VMware vSphere or Microsoft Hyper-V to consolidate physical servers into virtual machines (VMs), optimizing resource utilization and simplifying management.

Network Virtualization: Utilize network virtualization technologies like Virtual Extensible LAN (VXLAN) or Network Virtualization using Generic Routing Encapsulation (NVGRE) to create logical networks and enable workload mobility across physical network boundaries.

Storage Virtualization: Leverage storage virtualization technologies like Storage Area Network (SAN) virtualization or Network-Attached Storage (NAS) virtualization to centralize and optimize storage management.

Designing for Virtualized Network Environments:

Designing networks for virtualized environments requires considerations specific to virtualization. Consider the following design practices:

Network Bandwidth and Capacity Planning: Account for the increased network traffic and bandwidth requirements resulting from VM migrations, inter-VM communication, and data transfers within the virtualized environment.

Network Segmentation and Isolation: Design virtual LANs (VLANs) or virtual networks to segment and isolate traffic between VMs or groups of VMs, ensuring security and performance.

Network Hypervisor Integration: Integrate network hypervisor technologies, such as Cisco Nexus 1000V, to extend network policies, security, and management features to the virtualized environment.

Cloud Computing and Network Design Considerations:

Cloud computing enables on-demand access to computing resources, applications, and services. Consider the following design considerations for cloud environments:

Cloud Service Models: Understand the different cloud service models - Infrastructure as a Service (IaaS), Platform as a Service (PaaS), and Software as a Service (SaaS) - and design networks to support the selected cloud model.

Scalability and Elasticity: Design networks that can scale horizontally to accommodate increased resource demands and provide elastic network services to adapt to fluctuating workloads.

Hybrid and Multi-Cloud Networks: Plan and design networks that seamlessly integrate private and public cloud resources to create hybrid cloud environments. Consider interconnecting multiple clouds to enable workload mobility and ensure redundancy.

Cloud Security: Implement robust security measures like encryption, access controls, and data protection mechanisms to ensure the confidentiality, integrity, and availability of data in cloud environments.

Network Orchestration and Automation:

Network orchestration and automation streamline the deployment, management, and provisioning of network resources. Consider the following aspects:

Software-Defined Networking (SDN): Understand SDN concepts and design networks that leverage SDN controllers and programmable network devices for centralized management and control.

Automation Tools: Utilize network automation tools like Ansible, Puppet, or Cisco DNA Center to automate network configuration, provisioning, and monitoring tasks, improving efficiency and reducing human error.

APIs and Scripting: Leverage APIs and scripting languages like Python to interact with network devices, automate network operations, and integrate network functions with other systems or applications.

Conclusion:

In this tutorial, we explored the design considerations for virtualization and cloud environments. By understanding virtualization technologies and concepts, designing for virtualized network environments, considering cloud computing and network design, and embracing network orchestration and automation, you can create efficient, scalable, and secure networks for virtualized and cloud environments.

In the next chapter, we will focus on network automation and programmability, including the importance of network automation, software-defined networking (SDN), and APIs for network programmability. So, let's continue our journey to mastering CCDP certification and becoming skilled network designers!

Chapter 9: Network Automation and Programmability

Tutorial: Embracing Automation and Programmability in Network Design

Welcome to Chapter 9 of "Designing Networks with Confidence: A Comprehensive Guide to CCDP Exam Prep." In this chapter, we will explore the importance of network automation and programmability in network design. With the increasing complexity of networks, automation and programmability play a crucial role in improving efficiency, agility, and scalability. Let's dive into the key concepts and design practices!

Introduction to Network Automation and Programmability:

Network automation involves using software and tools to automate network operations, configuration, and management tasks. Programmability refers to the ability to configure and control network devices using programmable interfaces. Consider the following concepts:

Benefits of Network Automation: Understand the advantages of network automation, including reduced manual effort, improved consistency, faster deployment, and enhanced network reliability.

Programmable Interfaces: Learn about application programming interfaces (APIs) provided by network devices that allow programmability and interaction with network functions.

Software-Defined Networking (SDN): Explore the concept of SDN, which separates the control plane from the data plane, providing centralized management and control through programmable controllers.

Automation Tools and Technologies:

Discover various automation tools and technologies that facilitate network automation and programmability. Consider the following:

Configuration Management Tools: Utilize tools like Ansible, Chef, or Puppet for automating configuration tasks, ensuring consistency and scalability across network devices.

Network Orchestration Tools: Explore tools like Cisco DNA Center, Juniper Contrail, or VMware NSX to orchestrate network services, automate provisioning, and streamline network operations.

Network Monitoring and Analytics: Implement tools that provide real-time monitoring, performance analysis, and proactive alerting for efficient network management and troubleshooting.

Software-Defined Networking (SDN):

Understand the principles of SDN and its impact on network design. Consider the following design considerations:

SDN Controllers: Explore controller platforms such as OpenDaylight, Cisco Application Centric Infrastructure (ACI), or VMware NSX to centrally manage network policies, security, and service delivery.

Network Programmability: Leverage programmable network devices and SDN APIs to define network behavior, optimize traffic flows, and enable dynamic network configuration.

SDN Security: Implement security measures within the SDN framework to protect against unauthorized access, data breaches, and potential vulnerabilities.

APIs and Scripting for Network Automation:

Learn about the role of APIs and scripting in network automation and programmability. Consider the following aspects:

API Capabilities: Understand the capabilities of APIs provided by network devices, including configuration, monitoring, and data retrieval functionalities.

Scripting Languages: Explore scripting languages like Python to interact with APIs, automate network operations, and develop custom solutions for network automation.

Data Models: Discover standard data models like YANG and NETCONF that facilitate consistent and interoperable network programmability.

Network Automation Best Practices:

Adopt best practices for effective network automation and programmability. Consider the following design principles:

Define Clear Objectives: Clearly define automation goals and align them with business requirements, ensuring automation efforts address specific needs.

Start with Small Projects: Begin automation initiatives with smaller, well-defined projects to gain experience and build confidence in automation capabilities.

Test and Validate: Thoroughly test and validate automated configurations and scripts to ensure accuracy and minimize errors.

Collaboration and Documentation: Foster collaboration among teams and document automation processes, configurations, and troubleshooting steps for future reference.

Conclusion:

In this tutorial, we explored the importance of network automation and programmability in network design. By embracing automation tools, understanding SDN principles, leveraging APIs and scripting, and following best practices, you can streamline network operations, improve agility, and enhance scalability. Network automation and programmability are vital for managing complex networks efficiently.

In the final chapter, we will focus on exam preparation and practice, providing study techniques, exam format insights, and sample questions to help you prepare effectively for the CCDP exam. So, let's continue our journey to mastering CCDP certification and becoming skilled network designers!

Chapter 10: Exam Preparation and Practice

Tutorial: Mastering CCDP Exam Preparation

Welcome to the final chapter of "Designing Networks with Confidence: A Comprehensive Guide to CCDP Exam Prep." In this chapter, we will focus on exam preparation and practice to help you effectively prepare for the CCDP certification exam. Let's explore study techniques, exam format insights, and sample questions to maximize your success!

Understanding the CCDP Exam:

Before diving into exam preparation, it's essential to understand the structure and content of the CCDP exam. Consider the following aspects:

Exam Format: Familiarize yourself with the exam format, including the number and types of questions, time duration, and passing score requirements.

Exam Objectives: Review the official exam objectives provided by Cisco to gain a clear understanding of the topics covered in the exam. Ensure your study materials align with these objectives.

Study Techniques for Exam Preparation:

Effective study techniques can help you retain information and prepare for the exam efficiently. Consider the following techniques:

Create a Study Plan: Develop a study plan that outlines the topics to cover, study durations, and milestones to stay organized and focused.

Utilize Reliable Study Materials: Choose reputable study materials, such as Cisco Press books, official Cisco documentation, online courses, and practice exams, to ensure accurate and up-to-date content.

Hands-On Practice: Supplement your theoretical knowledge with hands-on practice using network simulation tools, virtual labs, or physical lab setups to reinforce concepts and gain practical experience.

Group Study and Discussion: Engage in group study or discussion forums to exchange ideas, clarify doubts, and deepen your understanding of complex topics.

Practice with Sample Questions:

Practice exams and sample questions provide valuable insights into the exam format and help you assess your readiness. Consider the following approaches:

Official Practice Exams: Access official Cisco practice exams, available on the Cisco Learning Network or through authorized training providers, to familiarize yourself with the question format and assess your knowledge.

Online Question Banks: Explore reputable online platforms that offer question banks specifically designed for the CCDP exam. Utilize these resources to gauge your understanding and identify areas for improvement.

Time Management: Practice answering questions within the allotted time to develop your time management skills and ensure you can complete the exam within the timeframe.

Exam-Day Strategies:

On the day of the exam, it's essential to approach the test with confidence and employ effective strategies. Consider the following strategies:

Read Instructions Carefully: Before starting the exam, read the instructions and question prompts thoroughly to understand the requirements and avoid any misunderstandings.

Answer Each Question: Even if you are unsure of the answer, attempt to answer each question as there is no penalty for guessing. Use the elimination method to narrow down options and make an educated guess if needed.

Time Management: Manage your time wisely throughout the exam to ensure you have sufficient time to answer all questions. If you encounter challenging questions, mark them for review and move on, returning to them later if time permits.

Review Your Answers: After completing all the questions, use the remaining time to review your answers, double-check for any errors, and ensure you haven't missed any questions.

Stay Calm and Focused: Maintain a calm and focused mindset during the exam. If you encounter difficult questions, take a deep breath, eliminate distractions, and approach them systematically.

Conclusion:

In this tutorial, we explored exam preparation and practice techniques to help you master the CCDP certification exam. By understanding the exam structure, utilizing effective study techniques, practicing with sample questions, and employing exam-day strategies, you can enhance your readiness and confidence for the exam.

Remember, diligent preparation, thorough understanding of exam objectives, and practical hands-on experience are key to succeeding in the CCDP exam. Best of luck with your exam, and congratulations on your journey to becoming a skilled network designer!

Chapter 11: Beyond the Exam: Continued Learning and Professional Growth

Tutorial: Nurturing Your Skills as a Network Designer

Welcome to Chapter 11 of "Designing Networks with Confidence: A Comprehensive Guide to CCDP Exam Prep." In this final chapter, we will explore the importance of continued learning and professional growth as a network designer beyond the CCDP exam. Network design is an ever-evolving field, and nurturing your skills is crucial for staying up-to-date and advancing your career. Let's delve into strategies for ongoing learning and professional development!

Stay Informed with Industry Trends:

Keeping up with the latest industry trends and advancements is essential for network designers. Consider the following strategies:

Networking Communities: Engage with professional networking communities, forums, and social media groups focused on network design. Participate in discussions, share knowledge, and learn from industry peers.

Industry Events and Conferences: Attend industry conferences, seminars, and webinars to gain insights into emerging technologies, best practices, and industry trends. Network with experts and explore new ideas.

Continuous Research: Dedicate time to independent research, reading industry publications, whitepapers, and blogs to stay informed about the latest developments in network design and related technologies.

Pursue Advanced Certifications:

While achieving the CCDP certification is a significant accomplishment, consider pursuing advanced certifications to further enhance your skills and expand your expertise. Consider the following certifications:

Cisco Certified Internetwork Expert (CCIE): This expert-level certification focuses on advanced networking knowledge and hands-on skills. It demonstrates a deep understanding of complex network design scenarios.

Certified Information Systems Security Professional (CISSP): This certification validates expertise in network security, aligning well with network design considerations for secure infrastructures.

Vendor-Specific Certifications: Explore additional certifications offered by networking vendors, such as Juniper Networks Certified Design Specialist (JNCDS) or Aruba Certified Design Expert (ACDX), to gain specialized knowledge in specific technologies.

Embrace Emerging Technologies:

Network design is heavily influenced by emerging technologies. Embracing these technologies will enable you to stay ahead of the curve. Consider the following areas:

Software-Defined Networking (SDN): Continue to explore SDN concepts, programmable networks, and SDN controllers to design and manage dynamic and scalable networks.

Cloud Networking: Deepen your understanding of cloud networking architectures, hybrid cloud environments, and integration strategies to effectively design networks for cloud-based infrastructures.

Internet of Things (IoT): Gain knowledge in IoT networking, including IoT protocols, device connectivity, and security considerations, as IoT continues to transform network design requirements.

Seek Continuous Skill Development:

Network design skills can be honed through continuous skill development. Consider the following strategies:

Hands-on Experience: Continue to gain practical experience through lab setups, network simulations, or virtualization technologies. Hands-on practice reinforces theoretical knowledge and enhances troubleshooting skills.

Mentorship and Collaboration: Seek mentorship from experienced network designers who can provide guidance and share insights. Collaborate with colleagues on projects to learn from their expertise and gain new perspectives.

Professional Development Programs: Explore professional development programs and workshops offered by industry organizations or training providers. These programs can provide structured learning opportunities and keep you updated on industry best practices.

Document and Share Your Expertise:

As you gain experience and knowledge, document your design methodologies, lessons learned, and best practices. Consider sharing your expertise through writing technical articles, blog posts, or presenting at industry events. Sharing your insights not only contributes to the community but also helps solidify your own understanding and expertise.

Conclusion:

In this tutorial, we explored strategies for continued learning and professional growth as a network designer beyond the CCDP exam. By staying informed with industry trends, pursuing advanced certifications, embracing emerging technologies, seeking continuous skill development, and documenting and sharing your expertise, you can nurture your skills, stay relevant, and advance your career in network design.

Remember, the field of network design is dynamic, and continuous learning is crucial to adapt to evolving technologies and industry demands. Embrace the journey of lifelong learning and seize opportunities for growth. Congratulations on your commitment to becoming a skilled network designer, and best wishes for a successful and fulfilling career!

Chapter 12: Case Studies in Network Design

Tutorial: Applying Network Design Principles to Real-World Scenarios

Welcome to Chapter 12 of "Designing Networks with Confidence: A Comprehensive Guide to CCDP Exam Prep." In this chapter, we will explore case studies in network design, where we will apply the principles and concepts learned throughout this book to real-world scenarios. By examining practical examples, you will gain a deeper understanding of how network design principles are applied in different contexts. Let's dive into the case studies!

Case Study 1: Campus Network Design:

In this case study, we will focus on designing a campus network for a large organization. Consider the following aspects:

Network Topology: Design a hierarchical network topology that accommodates multiple buildings or departments, providing scalability and ease of management.

Redundancy and High Availability: Implement redundant links, devices, and power sources to ensure fault tolerance and uninterrupted operation.

VLAN Segmentation: Design VLANs to separate traffic and provide security and performance isolation between different user groups or departments.

Wireless Connectivity: Plan and design a robust wireless network to provide seamless connectivity across the campus, considering coverage, capacity, and security requirements.

Case Study 2: Data Center Network Design:

In this case study, we will focus on designing a data center network for a cloud service provider. Consider the following aspects:

Network Virtualization: Utilize network virtualization technologies like VXLAN or NVGRE to create logical networks and enable workload mobility within the data center.

Scalability and Flexibility: Design a highly scalable network architecture that can accommodate rapid growth and dynamic workload placement.

Network Security: Implement security measures such as micro-segmentation, firewalls, and intrusion detection/prevention systems to protect sensitive data and prevent unauthorized access.

Traffic Optimization: Utilize load balancing and traffic engineering techniques to ensure optimal resource utilization and efficient data flows within the data center.

Case Study 3: Branch Office Connectivity:

In this case study, we will focus on designing a network for branch office connectivity in a multinational company. Consider the following aspects:

Wide Area Network (WAN) Design: Select appropriate WAN technologies, such as MPLS or SD-WAN, to provide reliable and secure connectivity between branch offices and the central headquarters.

Quality of Service (QoS): Design QoS policies to prioritize critical applications and ensure sufficient bandwidth for real-time applications like voice or video conferencing.

Security and Compliance: Implement security measures like VPNs, next-generation firewalls, and access control mechanisms to protect data transmitted over the WAN and ensure compliance with industry regulations.

Backup and Redundancy: Plan for backup connectivity options, such as secondary WAN links or cellular backups, to ensure continuous branch office operations in case of primary link failures.

Case Study 4: Internet Service Provider (ISP) Network Design:

In this case study, we will focus on designing a network for an ISP that provides internet connectivity to residential and business customers. Consider the following aspects:

Border Gateway Protocol (BGP) Design: Implement BGP to connect to multiple upstream internet service providers and ensure efficient routing and redundancy.

Traffic Engineering: Utilize traffic engineering techniques like route manipulation and traffic prioritization to optimize traffic flows and ensure quality of service.

Denial of Service (DoS) Mitigation: Deploy DoS mitigation techniques, such as rate limiting, access control lists (ACLs), or scrubbing centers, to protect the network infrastructure from DoS attacks.

Network Monitoring and Management: Design a network management system that provides real-time monitoring, fault detection, and performance analysis to maintain the stability and reliability of the ISP network.

Conclusion:

In this tutorial, we explored case studies in network design, applying the principles and concepts learned throughout the book to real-world scenarios. By examining the design considerations for campus networks, data centers, branch office connectivity, and ISP networks, you gained practical insights into how network design principles are applied in different contexts.

Remember, each network design scenario is unique, and it's essential to adapt the design principles to meet specific requirements and constraints. By continuously refining your design skills and applying a systematic approach, you can create robust and efficient network architectures in various environments.

Congratulations on completing "Designing Networks with Confidence: A Comprehensive Guide to CCDP Exam Prep!" Best wishes in your future network design endeavors, and may you continue to excel in your career as a skilled network designer!

Chapter 13: Network Design Best Practices

Tutorial: Mastering Best Practices for Effective Network Design

Welcome to Chapter 13 of "Designing Networks with Confidence: A Comprehensive Guide to CCDP Exam Prep." In this chapter, we will explore network design best practices that are essential for creating efficient, scalable, and secure network architectures. By understanding and implementing these best practices, you will be equipped to design networks that meet the needs of modern organizations. Let's dive into the key principles!

Understand Business Requirements:

Before embarking on network design, it is crucial to thoroughly understand the business requirements and goals of the organization. Consider the following aspects:

Collaboration: Engage with stakeholders, including executives, IT staff, and end-users, to gather requirements and ensure alignment with business objectives.

Scalability: Anticipate future growth and design the network to accommodate increasing demands for bandwidth, users, and services.

Availability: Identify critical services and applications and design a network that ensures high availability and minimizes downtime.

Follow the Hierarchical Network Design Model:

The hierarchical network design model provides a structured approach for designing scalable networks. Consider the following layers:

Core Layer: The core layer provides high-speed connectivity and routing between different network segments. Design a core layer that offers high availability and low latency.

Distribution Layer: The distribution layer provides policy enforcement, filtering, and segmentation of network traffic. Design a distribution layer that facilitates efficient traffic distribution and implements security measures.

Access Layer: The access layer connects end-user devices to the network. Design an access layer that provides easy connectivity, supports various media types, and enforces access controls.

Implement Network Redundancy and Resiliency:

To ensure network availability and resilience, implement redundancy at various levels. Consider the following practices:

Redundant Links: Utilize link aggregation techniques, such as EtherChannel or Port Channel, to aggregate multiple physical links into logical high-bandwidth connections.

Redundant Devices: Deploy redundant network devices, such as switches, routers, or firewalls, to provide failover capabilities and ensure uninterrupted network operations.

Spanning Tree Protocol (STP): Configure STP or its variants, such as Rapid Spanning Tree Protocol (RSTP) or Multiple Spanning Tree Protocol (MSTP), to prevent network loops and provide loop-free redundant paths.

Optimize Network Security:

Network security is a critical consideration in any design. Implement comprehensive security measures to protect network assets. Consider the following practices:

Access Control: Utilize access control mechanisms, such as firewalls, VLAN segmentation, or role-based access control (RBAC), to control access to sensitive resources.

Intrusion Detection and Prevention Systems (IDPS): Deploy IDPS technologies to monitor network traffic, detect suspicious activities, and prevent potential attacks.

Secure Remote Access: Implement secure remote access technologies, such as VPNs with strong encryption and multifactor authentication, to protect network connections from unauthorized access.

Plan for Network Monitoring and Management:

Effective network monitoring and management are crucial for maintaining network performance and troubleshooting issues. Consider the following practices:

Network Monitoring Tools: Deploy network monitoring tools, such as network analyzers or SNMP-based monitoring systems, to gather real-time performance data and detect anomalies.

Log Management: Centralize and analyze logs generated by network devices and security systems to identify and mitigate security incidents or network performance issues.

Change Management: Implement a structured change management process to ensure proper documentation, validation, and testing of network changes to minimize disruptions and avoid configuration errors.

Conclusion:

In this tutorial, we explored network design best practices that are essential for creating efficient, scalable, and secure network architectures. By understanding business requirements, following the hierarchical design model, implementing network redundancy and resiliency, optimizing network security, and planning for network monitoring and management, you can design networks that meet the needs of modern organizations.

Remember, network design is an ongoing process, and it is crucial to continually reassess and adapt network designs to align with evolving business requirements and emerging technologies. By adhering to best practices, you can create robust and future-proof network infrastructures.

Congratulations on your journey to mastering CCDP certification and becoming a skilled network designer! May you apply these best practices to design networks that drive business success and empower organizations with reliable and secure connectivity.

Chapter 14: Network Design Documentation

Tutorial: Mastering Network Design Documentation

Welcome to Chapter 14 of "Designing Networks with Confidence: A Comprehensive Guide to CCDP Exam Prep." In this chapter, we will explore the importance of network design documentation and the key elements to consider when creating comprehensive design documentation. Effective documentation plays a crucial role in network design, implementation, and maintenance. Let's delve into the world of network design documentation!

Importance of Network Design Documentation:

Network design documentation serves as a vital reference for network engineers, administrators, and stakeholders involved in the design, implementation, and maintenance of the network infrastructure. Consider the following reasons why documentation is essential:

Communication: Documentation provides a clear and standardized way to communicate design decisions, configurations, and best practices to the entire network team.

Knowledge Transfer: Well-documented designs ensure smooth knowledge transfer between team members, enabling efficient troubleshooting, maintenance, and future enhancements.

Compliance and Auditing: Documentation serves as evidence of compliance with industry standards, regulations, and internal policies. It facilitates auditing processes and ensures proper governance.

Scalability and Evolution: Design documentation provides a foundation for scalability, as it allows future network enhancements and modifications to be planned and implemented with minimal disruption.

Key Elements of Network Design Documentation:

When creating network design documentation, consider including the following key elements:

Executive Summary: Provide a high-level overview of the network design, highlighting its objectives, benefits, and key features. This section is crucial for conveying the design's value to stakeholders.

Network Topology Diagrams: Include detailed network topology diagrams that illustrate the physical and logical components of the network, including devices, connections, and VLANs.

IP Addressing and Subnetting Scheme: Document the IP addressing scheme, including subnets, VLAN assignments, and any reserved IP ranges. This information helps with IP management and troubleshooting.

Device Inventory: Maintain an inventory of network devices, including their make, model, serial numbers, and firmware versions. This inventory aids in tracking and managing the network infrastructure.

Configuration Files: Capture and store the configuration files of network devices, such as routers, switches, and firewalls. These files are invaluable for disaster recovery, device replacement, and troubleshooting.

Security Policies and Access Controls: Document the security policies, access control lists (ACLs), and firewall rules that govern network access and protect sensitive resources.

Performance and Capacity Planning: Include performance and capacity planning details, such as expected network traffic patterns, bandwidth requirements, and scalability considerations.

Documenting Design Rationale and Assumptions:

To provide context and justification for design decisions, it is crucial to document the rationale and assumptions behind the network design. Consider the following elements:

Design Goals: Clearly state the design goals, including scalability, availability, security, and performance requirements, to provide a framework for decision-making.

Design Constraints: Identify and document any constraints that influenced the design, such as budget limitations, regulatory requirements, or existing infrastructure limitations.

Design Trade-offs: Explain any design trade-offs made to balance conflicting requirements, such as security versus usability or cost versus performance.

Assumptions and Dependencies: Document any assumptions made during the design process, such as assumptions about future growth, user behavior, or third-party integrations.

Updating and Maintaining Documentation:

Network design documentation should not be static; it should evolve with the network. Consider the following practices for updating and maintaining documentation:

Change Management: Implement a change management process to ensure that documentation is updated whenever changes are made to the network design or configurations.

Version Control: Maintain version control of design documentation to track changes over time and ensure that the latest version is readily accessible to the network team.

Regular Reviews: Schedule regular reviews of design documentation to validate its accuracy, relevance, and alignment with the current network infrastructure.

Knowledge Sharing: Foster a culture of knowledge sharing within the network team by encouraging team members to contribute to and update the documentation as they gain insights and expertise.

Conclusion:

In this tutorial, we explored the importance of network design documentation and the key elements to consider when creating comprehensive design documentation. By understanding the significance of documentation, including network topology diagrams, IP addressing schemes, configuration files, security policies, and design rationale, you can ensure effective communication, knowledge transfer, compliance, and scalability within your network infrastructure.

Remember, network design documentation is a living artifact that should be regularly updated and maintained to reflect the evolving network environment. By maintaining accurate and comprehensive documentation, you empower your network team and stakeholders to effectively manage, troubleshoot, and enhance the network infrastructure.

Congratulations on your journey to mastering CCDP certification and becoming a skilled network designer! May your network design documentation be a valuable resource that enables efficient network operations and promotes successful business outcomes.

Chapter 15: Network Design Validation and Testing

Tutorial: Ensuring the Reliability of Network Designs

Welcome to Chapter 15 of "Designing Networks with Confidence: A Comprehensive Guide to CCDP Exam Prep." In this chapter, we will explore the importance of network design validation and testing and discuss the key strategies and techniques to ensure the reliability and effectiveness of network designs. By validating and testing your designs, you can identify and address potential issues before deployment. Let's dive into the world of network design validation and testing!

Importance of Network Design Validation:

Network design validation is a critical step to ensure that the proposed design meets the requirements and functions as intended. Consider the following reasons why network design validation is important:

Identify Design Flaws: Validation helps identify design flaws, such as scalability limitations, performance bottlenecks, or security vulnerabilities, before they impact the live network.

Verify Functionality: By validating the design, you can ensure that all required features and functionality, such as routing protocols, security policies, or quality of service (QoS) mechanisms, are properly implemented.

Optimize Performance: Validation allows you to assess the performance of the network design under different conditions, ensuring that it can handle the expected traffic load and meet performance targets.

Strategies for Network Design Validation:

To effectively validate network designs, consider the following strategies:

Simulation and Modeling: Utilize network simulation tools, such as Cisco Packet Tracer, GNS3, or EVE-NG, to create virtual environments that mimic the proposed network design. Simulations help evaluate network behavior, performance, and interactions between different components.

Proof of Concept (PoC): Implement a proof of concept by deploying a scaled-down version of the network design in a controlled environment. This allows you to validate specific design aspects, test configurations, and assess the overall functionality.

Peer Review: Seek feedback from peers, colleagues, or subject matter experts to obtain different perspectives and identify potential design issues or improvements. Peer review provides valuable insights and helps validate the design against industry best practices.

Network Design Testing Techniques:

In addition to validation, comprehensive testing is crucial to ensure the reliability and performance of network designs. Consider the following testing techniques:

Functional Testing: Validate the functionality of individual network components, such as routers, switches, or firewalls, to ensure they operate as intended. This includes testing protocols, routing tables, access control lists (ACLs), and other configuration parameters.

Performance Testing: Assess the performance of the network design by generating simulated traffic to evaluate factors like throughput, latency, packet loss, and capacity. Performance testing helps identify potential bottlenecks and performance limitations.

Security Testing: Conduct security testing to assess the effectiveness of security measures, such as firewalls, intrusion detection systems, or access controls. This includes vulnerability scanning, penetration testing, and assessing the network's resilience to attacks.

Failover and Redundancy Testing: Validate the failover mechanisms and redundancy configurations to ensure that the network design can gracefully handle device or link failures without significant impact on network operations.

Documenting Validation and Testing Results:

To maintain a record of the validation and testing process, it is crucial to document the results. Consider the following practices:

Test Plans: Develop comprehensive test plans that outline the objectives, methodologies, and expected outcomes of each validation or testing activity. Test plans provide a structured approach and help ensure thorough coverage.

Test Results: Document the results of each validation or testing activity, including observations, issues encountered, and actions taken to address them. This documentation serves as a reference for future troubleshooting or design modifications.

Lessons Learned: Capture lessons learned during the validation and testing process to continuously improve the design and testing approach in future projects. These insights contribute to the overall knowledge base and facilitate ongoing learning.

Conclusion:

In this tutorial, we explored the importance of network design validation and testing, as well as the key strategies and techniques to ensure the reliability and effectiveness of network designs. By validating the design against requirements, leveraging simulation and modeling tools, conducting functional, performance, security, and failover testing, and documenting the results, you can identify and address potential issues before deployment.

Remember, network design validation and testing are iterative processes. As you uncover issues or make design modifications, it is crucial to re-validate and re-test to ensure the desired outcomes. By dedicating time and effort to validation and testing, you can have confidence in the reliability and performance of your network designs.

Congratulations on your journey to mastering CCDP certification and becoming a skilled network designer! May your network designs be validated and tested to perfection,

providing reliable and efficient connectivity for your
organization.

Chapter 16: Network Design Troubleshooting

Tutorial: Mastering Network Design Troubleshooting Techniques

Welcome to Chapter 16 of "Designing Networks with Confidence: A Comprehensive Guide to CCDP Exam Prep." In this chapter, we will explore network design troubleshooting techniques to help you effectively diagnose and resolve issues that may arise in network designs. Troubleshooting is a critical skill for network designers, as it ensures the smooth operation and performance of network infrastructures. Let's delve into the world of network design troubleshooting!

Importance of Network Design Troubleshooting:

Network design troubleshooting is essential to identify and resolve issues that can impact the functionality, performance, and security of network designs. Consider the following reasons why network design troubleshooting is important:

Issue Identification: Troubleshooting helps identify and isolate issues in the network design, such as connectivity problems, performance bottlenecks, or misconfigurations, to ensure optimal network operation.

Problem Resolution: By systematically troubleshooting network issues, you can determine the root cause and implement the necessary corrective actions to resolve the problems effectively.

Minimize Downtime: Timely and efficient troubleshooting minimizes network downtime, reducing the impact on end-users and enabling the network to meet business requirements.

Troubleshooting Methodology:

To approach network design troubleshooting systematically, follow a structured troubleshooting methodology. Consider the following steps:

Gather Information: Begin by collecting relevant information about the issue, including error messages, symptoms, recent changes, and affected network devices or segments. Consult network monitoring tools, logs, or reports to gain insights.

Define the Problem: Clearly define the problem statement based on the gathered information. Understand the expected behavior, identify the deviation from that behavior, and define the impact on the network.

Identify Potential Causes: Generate a list of potential causes based on the defined problem. Consider factors such as misconfigurations, hardware failures, software bugs, or external factors like environmental conditions or network congestion.

Isolate and Test: Begin isolating the potential causes by performing targeted tests and diagnostics. Use network diagnostic tools, such as ping, traceroute, or packet captures, to verify connectivity, analyze network traffic, and identify points of failure.

Resolve the Issue: Once the root cause is identified, implement the necessary corrective actions to resolve the issue. This may involve reconfiguring devices, updating firmware, replacing faulty components, or adjusting network parameters.

Validate and Document: After resolving the issue, validate the network's behavior to ensure the problem is fully resolved. Document the troubleshooting steps taken, including the identified root cause and the implemented solution, for future reference.

Troubleshooting Tools and Techniques:

To facilitate effective network design troubleshooting, consider the following tools and techniques:

Network Monitoring Tools: Utilize network monitoring tools, such as SNMP-based systems or performance management platforms, to gain real-time visibility into network traffic, device health, and performance metrics.

Diagnostic Tools: Leverage network diagnostic tools, including ping, traceroute, network analyzers, or protocol analyzers, to analyze network traffic, pinpoint connectivity issues, and troubleshoot protocol-related problems.

Configuration Auditing: Perform regular configuration audits to ensure consistency and compliance with design best practices. Configuration auditing tools help identify misconfigurations or discrepancies between the design and the actual configurations.

Collaboration and Knowledge Sharing: Foster collaboration among network teams, subject matter experts, and vendors to leverage collective knowledge and experience when troubleshooting complex issues. Sharing insights and collaborating on troubleshooting efforts can lead to faster resolutions.

Troubleshooting Common Network Design Issues:

While network design issues can vary widely, certain common issues are frequently encountered. Consider the following troubleshooting techniques for common network design issues:

Connectivity Problems: Verify physical connections, check link status, and troubleshoot routing or switching issues to resolve connectivity problems.

Performance Bottlenecks: Analyze network traffic, identify bandwidth-intensive applications, optimize network QoS parameters, and implement traffic engineering techniques to alleviate performance bottlenecks.

Security Vulnerabilities: Conduct security assessments, review access control mechanisms, and perform vulnerability scanning and penetration testing to identify and address security vulnerabilities.

Protocol or Service Issues: Analyze protocol-specific behaviors, verify configuration parameters, and troubleshoot protocol-related issues using protocol analyzers or debugging tools.

Conclusion:

In this tutorial, we explored network design troubleshooting techniques to help you effectively diagnose and resolve issues that may arise in network designs. By following a structured troubleshooting methodology, utilizing appropriate tools and techniques, and collaborating with stakeholders, you can efficiently troubleshoot network issues and ensure the smooth operation of network designs.

Remember, troubleshooting requires a systematic approach, attention to detail, and continuous learning. As you encounter different network issues and challenges, you will develop a deeper understanding of troubleshooting techniques and gain expertise in resolving complex design-related problems.

Congratulations on your journey to mastering CCDP certification and becoming a skilled network designer! May your troubleshooting skills be sharp and your network designs thrive with optimal performance and reliability.

Chapter 17: Network Design Optimization

Tutorial: Mastering Network Design Optimization Techniques

Welcome to Chapter 17 of "Designing Networks with Confidence: A Comprehensive Guide to CCDP Exam Prep." In this chapter, we will explore network design optimization techniques to help you enhance the performance, efficiency, and scalability of network designs. Optimization plays a crucial role in ensuring that network infrastructures meet evolving business requirements and deliver the desired outcomes. Let's delve into the world of network design optimization!

Importance of Network Design Optimization:

Network design optimization aims to improve the overall performance, efficiency, and scalability of network infrastructures. Consider the following reasons why network design optimization is important:

Enhanced Performance: Optimization techniques help maximize network performance by minimizing latency, reducing packet loss, and improving throughput.

Improved Efficiency: Optimization ensures efficient utilization of network resources, such as bandwidth, memory, or processing power, resulting in cost savings and better resource management.

Scalability: Optimized network designs can accommodate growth and scalability requirements, allowing networks to expand seamlessly as the organization evolves.

Optimization Techniques for Network Design:

To optimize network designs, consider the following techniques:

Traffic Engineering: Implement traffic engineering techniques, such as load balancing, traffic prioritization, or Quality of Service (QoS), to optimize network traffic flows and ensure optimal resource allocation based on application requirements.

Routing Optimization: Optimize routing protocols, such as OSPF or BGP, by fine-tuning parameters, configuring route summarization, or utilizing route filters to minimize convergence time, reduce routing table size, and improve routing efficiency.

Network Segmentation: Segmenting networks using VLANs, virtual routing and forwarding (VRF), or network virtualization techniques helps optimize network performance, improve security, and facilitate efficient resource allocation.

Protocol Optimization: Fine-tune protocol parameters and configurations to optimize protocol behaviors. For example, optimizing spanning tree protocol timers or adjusting EIGRP or OSPF metric calculations can enhance convergence and performance.

Bandwidth Management: Implement bandwidth management techniques, such as traffic shaping, rate limiting, or queuing mechanisms, to prioritize critical traffic, manage bandwidth utilization, and prevent network congestion.

Optimization Considerations for Specific Network Domains:

Optimization techniques may vary depending on specific network domains. Consider the following optimization considerations for different network domains:

Data Center Optimization: Optimize data center network designs by implementing technologies like virtual port channels (vPC), overlay networks, or data center interconnect (DCI) solutions to enhance scalability, performance, and workload mobility.

Wide Area Network (WAN) Optimization: Utilize WAN optimization techniques, such as data compression, caching, or traffic prioritization, to optimize bandwidth utilization, reduce latency, and enhance application performance across geographically distributed sites.

Wireless Network Optimization: Optimize wireless network designs by fine-tuning access point placement, channel selection, power settings, and authentication mechanisms to improve coverage, capacity, and client connectivity.

Cloud Network Optimization: Optimize cloud network designs by leveraging cloud-specific technologies and architectures, such as virtual private clouds (VPCs), direct cloud connectivity, or content delivery networks (CDNs), to enhance performance, security, and cost-efficiency.

Continuous Monitoring and Optimization:

Network optimization is an ongoing process that requires continuous monitoring and evaluation. Consider the following practices:

Network Monitoring: Utilize network monitoring tools to gather real-time performance data, analyze network traffic patterns, and identify areas for optimization.

Baseline Establishment: Establish performance baselines for critical network metrics, such as latency, throughput, or response times, to track changes and identify deviations that may require optimization.

Regular Assessments: Perform regular assessments of network designs, including capacity planning, security audits, and performance evaluations, to identify optimization opportunities and address potential bottlenecks.

Feedback Loop: Encourage feedback from network users, administrators, and stakeholders to gather insights and identify areas that require optimization. Engage in continuous improvement efforts based on feedback received.

Conclusion:

In this tutorial, we explored network design optimization techniques to help you enhance the performance, efficiency, and scalability of network designs. By leveraging optimization techniques like traffic engineering, routing optimization, network segmentation, and protocol optimization, you can optimize network infrastructures to meet evolving business requirements.

Remember, network optimization is an ongoing process that requires continuous monitoring, evaluation, and adaptation. By staying attuned to network performance metrics, assessing network designs regularly, and engaging in continuous improvement efforts, you can ensure that your network designs deliver optimal performance and efficiency.

Congratulations on your journey to mastering CCDP certification and becoming a skilled network designer! May your network designs thrive with optimal performance, efficiency, and scalability, providing a solid foundation for business success.

Chapter 18: Network Design Documentation

Tutorial: Mastering Network Design Documentation

Welcome to Chapter 18 of "Designing Networks with Confidence: A Comprehensive Guide to CCDP Exam Prep." In this chapter, we will explore network design documentation in-depth. Documentation is a crucial aspect of network design as it ensures clear communication, facilitates collaboration, and enables effective management of network infrastructures. Let's dive into the world of network design documentation!

Importance of Network Design Documentation:

Network design documentation serves as a valuable resource for network engineers, administrators, and stakeholders involved in the design, implementation, and maintenance of network infrastructures. Consider the following reasons why network design documentation is important:

Communication: Documentation provides a standardized and clear means of communicating design decisions, configurations, and best practices to the entire network team.

Knowledge Transfer: Well-documented designs facilitate knowledge transfer between team members, ensuring smooth troubleshooting, maintenance, and future enhancements.

Compliance and Auditing: Documentation serves as evidence of compliance with industry standards, regulations, and internal policies, aiding in audits and ensuring proper governance.

Scalability and Evolution: Design documentation provides a foundation for scalability, allowing for planned growth and modifications to the network design in the future.

Key Elements of Network Design Documentation:

When creating network design documentation, consider including the following key elements:

Design Overview: Provide an overview of the network design, including its objectives, scope, and key features. This section helps stakeholders understand the purpose and value of the design.

Network Topology Diagrams: Include detailed network topology diagrams that depict the physical and logical components of the network, such as devices, connections, VLANs, and network segmentation.

IP Addressing Scheme: Document the IP addressing scheme, including subnets, VLAN assignments, and any reserved IP ranges. This information aids in IP management and troubleshooting.

Device Configuration Details: Capture the configuration details of network devices, including routers, switches, firewalls, and wireless access points. Include key settings, such as interfaces, routing protocols, security policies, and QoS configurations.

Security Policies and Access Controls: Document the security policies, access control lists (ACLs), and firewall rules that govern network access and protect sensitive resources.

Performance and Capacity Planning: Include performance and capacity planning details, such as expected network traffic patterns, bandwidth requirements, and scalability considerations.

Documenting Design Rationale and Assumptions:

To provide context and justification for design decisions, it is crucial to document the rationale and assumptions behind the network design. Consider the following elements:

Design Goals: Clearly state the design goals, including scalability, availability, security, and performance requirements, to provide a framework for decision-making.

Design Constraints: Identify and document any constraints that influenced the design, such as budget limitations, regulatory requirements, or existing infrastructure limitations.

Design Trade-offs: Explain any design trade-offs made to balance conflicting requirements, such as security versus usability or cost versus performance.

Assumptions and Dependencies: Document any assumptions made during the design process, such as assumptions about future growth, user behavior, or third-party integrations.

Updating and Maintaining Documentation:

Network design documentation should not be static; it should evolve with the network. Consider the following practices for updating and maintaining documentation:

Change Management: Implement a change management process to ensure that documentation is updated whenever changes are made to the network design or configurations.

Version Control: Maintain version control of design documentation to track changes over time and ensure that the latest version is readily accessible to the network team.

Regular Reviews: Schedule regular reviews of design documentation to validate its accuracy, relevance, and alignment with the current network infrastructure.

Knowledge Sharing: Foster a culture of knowledge sharing within the network team by encouraging team members to contribute to and update the documentation as they gain insights and expertise.

Tools for Network Design Documentation:

To streamline the documentation process, consider utilizing the following tools:

Diagramming Software: Use network diagramming software, such as Cisco Network Assistant, Microsoft Visio, or Lucidchart, to create professional and visually appealing network topology diagrams.

Collaboration Tools: Leverage collaboration platforms, such as Microsoft SharePoint, Google Drive, or Atlassian Confluence, to facilitate real-time collaboration, document sharing, and version control.

Documentation Templates: Utilize pre-designed documentation templates or develop your own standardized templates to ensure consistency and ease of use when documenting network designs.

Conclusion:

In this tutorial, we explored network design documentation in-depth, understanding its importance and the key elements to include when creating comprehensive design documentation. By emphasizing clear communication, knowledge transfer, compliance, and scalability, network design documentation becomes a valuable asset in managing and maintaining network infrastructures.

Remember, network design documentation is a living artifact that requires regular updates and maintenance. By adhering to best practices, implementing change management processes, leveraging version control, and fostering a culture of knowledge sharing, you ensure that your network design documentation remains accurate, relevant, and reliable.

Congratulations on your journey to mastering CCDP certification and becoming a skilled network designer! May your network design documentation serve as a valuable resource, promoting efficient collaboration, effective management, and successful network implementations.

Chapter 19: Network Design Review and Validation

Tutorial: Mastering Network Design Review and Validation

Welcome to Chapter 19 of "Designing Networks with Confidence: A Comprehensive Guide to CCDP Exam Prep." In this chapter, we will explore the process of network design review and validation. Reviewing and validating network designs is essential to ensure their effectiveness, adherence to best practices, and alignment with business requirements. Let's dive into the world of network design review and validation!

Importance of Network Design Review and Validation:

Network design review and validation are crucial steps in the network design process. They help identify design flaws, ensure adherence to industry best practices, and validate that the design meets the organization's requirements. Consider the following reasons why network design review and validation are important:

Quality Assurance: Reviewing and validating network designs help ensure their quality, reliability, and performance before implementation. It reduces the risk of costly rework or operational issues.

Best Practice Compliance: Design reviews help ensure that network designs follow industry best practices, design principles, and architectural standards. This promotes consistency and facilitates troubleshooting and maintenance.

Risk Mitigation: Validation identifies potential risks and vulnerabilities in the design, enabling proactive measures to address them before deployment. It helps prevent security breaches, performance bottlenecks, or scalability limitations.

Network Design Review Process:

To conduct a comprehensive network design review, consider the following steps:

Define Review Objectives: Clearly define the objectives and scope of the design review. Determine the key focus areas, such as scalability, security, performance, or compliance, based on the organization's requirements.

Gather Design Documentation: Collect all relevant design documentation, including network topology diagrams, IP addressing schemes, device configurations, security policies, and performance and capacity planning details.

Conduct Review Sessions: Engage network stakeholders, including network engineers, architects, administrators, and security experts, in review sessions. Evaluate the design against industry best practices, design principles, and organizational requirements.

Identify Design Flaws and Improvements: Analyze the design documentation and identify potential design flaws, scalability limitations, security vulnerabilities, or performance bottlenecks. Document recommended improvements or modifications to address these issues.

Document Review Findings: Record the findings of the design review, including identified issues, recommendations, and areas of improvement. Clearly communicate the findings to stakeholders, emphasizing the impact on network functionality, security, or performance.

Network Design Validation Process:

To validate the network design, consider the following steps:

Test Design Functionality: Validate the functionality of the network design by testing critical features and services, such as routing protocols, security policies, or Quality of Service (QoS) mechanisms. Ensure that the design meets the organization's requirements.

Perform Simulation or Proof of Concept: Utilize network simulation tools or implement a proof of concept to validate the design in a controlled environment. Test key design aspects, configurations, and scenarios to identify potential issues and evaluate performance.

Assess Performance and Scalability: Evaluate the performance of the network design under different loads, traffic patterns, and scenarios. Assess scalability to ensure the design can handle anticipated growth and changing requirements.

Conduct Security Assessments: Perform security assessments, such as vulnerability scanning, penetration testing, or compliance checks, to identify potential security risks or weaknesses. Ensure that the design aligns with industry best practices and security standards.

Validate Design Assumptions: Verify that the design assumptions made during the planning phase still hold true. Validate assumptions related to user behavior, application requirements, or third-party integrations to ensure design accuracy.

Iterative Nature of Design Review and Validation:

Design review and validation are iterative processes. As the network design evolves, it is important to conduct regular reviews and validations to ensure its ongoing effectiveness. Consider the following practices:

Change Management: Implement a change management process to review and validate design changes before implementation. Validate the impact of changes on network functionality, security, and performance.

Continuous Improvement: Encourage a culture of continuous improvement by incorporating feedback from design reviews and validations into future design iterations. Continuously seek opportunities to enhance the design based on lessons learned.

Documentation Updates: Update the design documentation based on review and validation findings. Maintain an accurate record of changes, recommendations, and improvements for future reference and knowledge sharing.

Conclusion:

In this tutorial, we explored the process of network design review and validation. By conducting design reviews, validating functionality and performance, and iteratively improving the design, you can ensure that network designs meet the organization's requirements, adhere to best practices, and mitigate potential risks.

Remember, network design review and validation are ongoing processes that should be integrated into the network design lifecycle. By incorporating regular review and validation activities, you can maintain the quality, reliability, and effectiveness of network designs.

Congratulations on your journey to mastering CCDP certification and becoming a skilled network designer! May your network designs undergo thorough review and validation, resulting in robust, secure, and high-performing network infrastructures.

Chapter 20: Network Design Documentation Templates and Best Practices

Tutorial: Creating Effective Network Design Documentation

Welcome to Chapter 20 of "Designing Networks with Confidence: A Comprehensive Guide to CCDP Exam Prep." In this chapter, we will explore network design documentation templates and best practices. Effective documentation is crucial for clear communication, efficient troubleshooting, and successful network management. By following documentation templates and best practices, you can create comprehensive and organized network design documentation. Let's delve into the world of network design documentation templates and best practices!

Importance of Network Design Documentation Templates:

Network design documentation templates provide a standardized structure and format for documenting network designs. They ensure consistency, ease of understanding, and efficient knowledge transfer among network teams. Consider the following reasons why using documentation templates is important:

Consistency: Templates enforce a consistent structure and format across different network design documents, making them easier to read and comprehend.

Efficiency: Templates save time and effort by providing predefined sections and headings, reducing the need to start from scratch for each new document.

Completeness: Templates ensure that all relevant information is captured in the documentation, minimizing the risk of missing critical details.

Standardization: By using templates, network designs can be consistently documented across different projects and network environments, enhancing collaboration and troubleshooting.

Key Elements of Network Design Documentation Templates:

When creating network design documentation templates, consider including the following key elements:

Cover Page: Include a cover page with the document title, version, date, and the names of the author(s) and reviewers.

Table of Contents: Provide a table of contents with hyperlinks to quickly navigate to different sections of the document.

Executive Summary: Summarize the network design objectives, key features, and benefits in a concise manner to provide a high-level overview.

Design Overview: Describe the purpose, scope, and goals of the network design, highlighting its alignment with business requirements.

Network Topology Diagrams: Include clear and labeled network topology diagrams depicting the physical and logical components of the network design.

IP Addressing and Subnetting: Document the IP addressing scheme, subnet allocations, VLAN assignments, and any reserved IP ranges.

Device Inventory: List all network devices involved in the design, including their make, model, serial numbers, and firmware versions.

Configuration Templates: Provide pre-defined configuration templates or placeholders for network devices, helping ensure consistent and standardized configurations.

Security Policies and Access Controls: Detail the security policies, access control lists (ACLs), and firewall rules that govern network access and protect sensitive resources.

Performance and Capacity Planning: Include performance and capacity planning details, such as expected network traffic patterns, bandwidth requirements, and scalability considerations.

Best Practices for Network Design Documentation:

In addition to using templates, consider the following best practices when creating network design documentation:

Clear and Concise Language: Use clear and concise language to ensure easy comprehension of the document. Avoid technical jargon or unnecessary complexity.

Detailed Descriptions: Provide detailed descriptions of design decisions, configurations, and assumptions to aid understanding and troubleshooting.

Organization and Structure: Organize the document logically, using headings, subheadings, and sections to improve readability and navigation.

Consistent Formatting: Maintain consistent formatting throughout the document, including font styles, font sizes, bullet points, and numbering.

Revision History: Include a revision history section to track document changes, versions, and the names of individuals who made revisions.

Document Versioning: Use a versioning system, such as date-based or numerical, to track document versions and revisions accurately.

Visual Aids: Incorporate visual aids, such as screenshots, diagrams, or tables, to illustrate complex concepts and enhance understanding.

Regular Updates: Regularly review and update the documentation to ensure its accuracy, relevance, and alignment with the current network design.

Document Control and Accessibility:

To ensure document control and accessibility, consider the following practices:

Document Storage: Store network design documentation in a centralized and secure location, such as a document management system or a shared network drive.

Access Permissions: Define access permissions and restrictions to ensure that only authorized individuals can view, edit, or share the documentation.

Version Control: Implement version control mechanisms to track changes, maintain document history, and ensure that the latest version is readily accessible to the network team.

Backups and Redundancy: Regularly back up network design documentation to prevent data loss and ensure redundancy in case of system failures or accidents.

Conclusion:

In this tutorial, we explored network design documentation templates and best practices to help you create effective and comprehensive network design documentation. By using templates, including key elements, following best practices, and maintaining document control and accessibility, you can produce organized, consistent, and valuable documentation.

Remember, network design documentation serves as a critical reference for network teams, stakeholders, and future troubleshooting or enhancements. By investing time and effort into creating high-quality documentation, you contribute to efficient communication, effective management, and successful network designs.

Congratulations on your journey to mastering CCDP certification and becoming a skilled network designer! May your network design documentation be well-structured, informative, and accessible, enabling seamless collaboration and successful network implementations.

www.ingramcontent.com/pod-product-compliance
Lightning Source LLC
LaVergne TN
LVHW022125060326
832903LV00063B/4060